AN APPEAL BY THE

DALAI LAMA

TO THE WORLD

FSC
www.fsc.org
MIX
Papier aus verantwortungsvollen Quellen
FSC® C012536

First edition 2016

Owner, publisher, and responsible for content:
Red Bull Media House GmbH
Oberst-Lepperdinger-Strasse 11–15
5071 Wals near Salzburg, Austria
More information at:
www.redbullmediahouse.com
www.beneventobooks.com

Cover design and typography: Frank Behrendt, Peter Feierabend
Cover photo, page 4: Bigi Alt
English translation: Jake Schneider
Printed by: Buch.Bücher Theiss, www.theiss.at

ISBN 978-3-7109-0006-8

AN APPEAL BY THE DALAI LAMA TO THE WORLD

WITH FRANZ ALT

Ethics Are More Important Than Religion

BENEVENTO

PREFACE

»I DON'T HAVE ANY ENEMIES«

»I don't have any enemies, only people I haven't met yet,« the Dalai Lama told me over 20 years ago. He also said, »We have the most to learn from our enemies. In a way, they are our best teachers.« So wise and yet so realistic are the words of the most prominent refugee in the world – and also one of the oldest – after 56 years of exile in India. Even though he has been forced to live outside his Chinese-occupied homeland since 1959, he does not harbor any hatred of Chinese people or their leadership. On the contrary, he sometimes calls himself a »Communist Buddhist« or a »Buddhist Communist« and says he even prays for the Communist leaders in Beijing, adding with a laugh, »In Europe I would vote for the Green party, because the problem of the environment is a question of our survival.«

Over the course of 33 years, we have met over 30 times and had 15 television interviews. Rarely have I encountered such an empathetic interview subject or one so full of humor. None of them has laughed more than he has. It is no coincidence that he has been voted the nicest person in the world in surveys. Over the last few years, the Dalai Lama has come to consider ethics across religious divisions to be more and more important. And today he goes a step further, making a statement unparalleled for a religious leader: »Ethics are more important than religion. We are not members of a particular religion at birth. But ethics are innate.« In the talks he gives worldwide, he refers to »secular ethics beyond all religions« with growing frequency. Albert Schweitzer had another term for the same concept: »reverence for life.«

The Dalai Lama's secular ethics transcend national, religious, and cultural boundaries and define values that are innate in all people and apply to everyone alike. Rather than superficial, material values, these are inner values such as mindfulness, compassion, training the mind, and the pursuit of happiness. »If we want to be happy ourselves, we should practice compassion, and if we want other people to be happy, we should likewise practice compassion. All of us would rather see smiling faces than frowning ones,« he says.

One of the Dalai Lama's central beliefs is this: all people are united in our pursuit of happiness and our desire to avoid suffering. This is the source of humanity's greatest achievements. For that reason, we should begin to think and act on the basis of an identity rooted in the words »we humans.«

The Dalai Lama believes that without secular ethics, we cannot solve all the problems we face: wars in the Middle East, Ukraine, Somalia, and North Africa, 20 million global refugees, civil wars in Nigeria and Afghanistan, climate change and the environmental crisis, the global financial crisis, and world hunger. He explains and elaborates his revolutionary assertions in the conversation to follow. What the Dalai Lama suggests is a revolution of empathy and compassion – a revolution combining all previous revolutions. Without empathy and compassion, evolution would not have happened in the first place.

In January 2015, appalled at the Islamist terrorist attack at the editorial offices of the satirical newspaper *Charlie Hebdo* and a Jewish supermarket in Paris, the Dalai Lama said, »On some days I think it would be better if there were no religions. All religions and all scriptures harbor potential for violence. That is why we need secular ethics beyond all religions. It is more important for schools to have classes on ethics than religion. Why? Because it's more important for humanity's survival to be aware of our commonalities than to constantly emphasize what divides us.« This insight was the spark for the interview that follows.

Here is a new message that can change the world.

On 6 July 2015, the Nobel Peace Prize laureate will be 80 years old. To mark that occasion, this little book is being published in every major world language at once.

Franz Alt
Baden-Baden, Germany, March 2015

Appeal by the Dalai Lama for Secular Ethics and Peace

For thousands of years, violence has been committed and justified in the name of religion. Religions have often been intolerant and still are in many cases. Religion is often abused or exploited – even by religious leaders – in order to further political or economic interests. For that reason I say that in the twenty-first century, we need a new form of ethics beyond religion. I am speaking of a secular ethics that can be helpful and useful for over a billion atheists and an increasing number of agnostics. More integral than religion is our fundamental human spirituality. That is the affinity we humans have for love, benevolence, and affection – no matter what religion we belong to.

I believe that humans can get by without religion, but not without inner values, not without ethics. The difference between ethics and religion is like the difference between water and tea. Religion-based ethics and inner values are more like water. The tea that we drink is made mostly of water, but it contains other ingredients as well – tea leaves, spices, perhaps a little sugar, and, at least in Tibet, a pinch of salt – and that makes it more substantial, more lasting, something we want to drink every day. Yet no matter how tea is prepared, its main ingredient is always water. We can live without tea, but not without water. Likewise, we are born without religion, but not without the basic need for compassion – and not without the fundamental need for water.

I see with ever greater clarity that our spiritual well-being depends not on religion, but on our innate human nature, our natural affinity for goodness, compassion, and caring for others. Regardless of whether or not we belong to a religion, we all have a fundamental and profoundly human wellspring of ethics within ourselves. We need to nurture that shared ethical basis. Ethics, as opposed to religion, are grounded in human nature. And that is how we can work on preserving creation. That is religion and ethics put into practice. Empathy is the basis of human coexistence. It is my belief that human development relies on cooperation and not competition. That is scientifically proven.

We must learn now that humanity is all one big family. We are all brothers and sisters: physically, mentally, and emotionally. But we are still focusing far too much on our differences instead of our commonalities. After all, every one of us is born the same way and dies the same way. It doesn't make much sense to take pride in our nations and religions – all the way to the graveyard!

Ethics run deeper and are more natural than religion.

Climate change, too, can only be solved on a global scale. I hope and pray that this realization will finally bring tangible results at the next climate summit in Paris in late 2015. Egotism, nationalism, and violence are the fundamentally incorrect path.

The most important question we can ask for a better world is »How can we serve each other?« To make that shift, we need to sharpen our awareness. The same holds true for politicians. We need to maintain positive states of mind. I practice that four hours per day. Meditation is more important than ritualized prayer. Children should learn morals and ethics. That's more important than all religion.

The primary causes of war and violence are our negative emotions. We give them too much space and give too little space to our intellects and our compassion.

I suggest more listening, more contemplation, more meditation. I agree with Mahatma Gandhi: »Be the change you want to see in the world.«

In some totalitarian countries, we see that peace can only last if human rights are respected, if people have food to eat, and if individuals and communities are free. We can only achieve true peace within, among, and around ourselves by first achieving inner peace. Part of happiness is developing a universal sense of responsibility and a secular set of ethics.

I will always stand by nonviolence. That means intelligently loving your enemy. Through intensive meditation, we will find that our enemies can become our best friends. By following purely secular ethics, we will become more easygoing, empathetic, and judicious people. Then there is a chance for the twenty-first century to be a century of peace, a century of dialogue, and a century of a more caring, responsible, and empathetic human race.

That is my hope. And that is my prayer. I look forward with joy to the day when children will learn the principles of nonviolence and peaceful conflict resolution – in other words secular ethics – at school.

Far too much stock is placed in material values these days. They are important, but they will not solve our stress, anxiety, anger, or frustration. Still we must overcome our mental burdens such as stress, fear, anxiety, and frustration. That is why we need a deeper level of thinking. That is what I call mindfulness.

Through meditation and contemplation we can learn, for example, that patience is the most potent antidote for anger, satisfaction for greed, bravery for fear, and understanding for doubt. It is not very helpful to rage against others. Instead, we should strive to change ourselves.

Now humanity seems to be maturing somewhat. The desire for peace and the rejection of violence are very strong. We need to make worldwide efforts to stop, contain, or eliminate all violent methods. It is not enough anymore to tell people that we oppose violence and want peace.

We must use more effective methods. Arms exports are a major impediment to building peace.

Whenever we face difficulties or there is an economic crisis, or even when religious disputes arise, we must work towards a model where the only correct method is dialogue.

We must learn that we are all brothers and sisters. The past century was the century of violence.

This twenty-first century should be the century of dialogue! We can never change the past, but we can always learn from it to create a better future.

The idea that problems can be solved with violence and weapons is a disastrous delusion. With rare exceptions, violence always leads to more violence. In our interconnected world, war is an anachronism that contradicts reason and ethics. The Iraq War, which George W. Bush began in 2003, was a catastrophe. This conflict still hasn't been resolved to this day and has claimed the lives of many people.

It is plainly not enough to appeal to politicians' desire for peace. It is more important for increasing numbers of people throughout the world to speak out for disarmament. Disarmament is compassion put into practice. But the prerequisite for external disarmament is an inner disarmament of hatred, prejudice, and intolerance. I appeal to all current warring parties: »Don't arm yourselves! Disarm!« And to all people: »Overcome hatred and prejudice with understanding, cooperation, and tolerance!«

Notwithstanding all the suffering that China has brought upon us Tibetans for decades, I am deeply convinced that most human conflicts can be resolved through sincere dialogue. This strategy of nonviolence and reverence for all life is Tibet's gift to the world.

Dalai Lama
Dharamsala, India, March 2015

Ethics are more important than Religion

Franz Alt:

Your Holiness, my dear friend, after the terror attack in Paris in early January 2015, you spoke words that were provocative for a religious leader: »On some days I think it would be better if there were no religions!« You seem to be increasingly skeptical towards religions because they also bring violence, fanaticism, and intolerance. What did you mean by that?

Dalai Lama:

Religious knowledge and practice remain helpful, but they are no longer enough in the modern era. This is becoming clearer and clearer from many examples around the world. That applies to all religions, including Christianity and Buddhism of course. Wars are still waged in the name of religion and have even been called »holy wars.« For thousands of years, violence has been committed and justified in the name of religion. Religions have often been intolerant and still are in many cases. For this reason I say that in the twenty-first century, we need a new form of ethics beyond religion. That is why I am speaking of secular ethics that can be helpful and useful for over a billion atheists and an increasing number of agnostics. More integral than religion is our fundamental human spirituality. That is the affinity we humans have for love, benevolence, and affection – no matter what religion we belong to.

Franz Alt:

Spirituality has become a fashionable word. What does it mean for you?

Dalai Lama:

Spirituality is the most fundamental of all human wellsprings inside us. When we decide to cultivate the inner values that we all appreciate in other people, we begin to live spiritually. We should create an ethical foundation and nurture our inner values to be appropriate to our scientific age without neglecting the deeper needs of the human spirit. Of course all religions can contribute to this holistic secular ethos.

I believe that humans can get by without religion, but not without inner values, not without ethics. The difference between ethics and religion is like the difference between water and tea. Religion-based ethics and inner values are more like water. The tea that we drink is made mostly of water, but it contains other ingredients as well – tea leaves, spices, perhaps a little sugar, and, at least in Tibet, a pinch of salt – and that makes it more substantial, more lasting, something we want to drink every day. Yet no matter how tea is prepared, its main ingredient is always water. We can live without tea, but not without water. Likewise, we are born without religion, but not without the basic need for compassion – and not without the fundamental need for water.

Franz Alt:

What gave you the idea that we in this era need more than the traditional religions?

Dalai Lama:

I've been living in exile in India for 56 years. There I have experienced secular ethics in practice and a secular society. Mahatma Gandhi was a deeply religious man but also a secular mind. In his daily rounds of prayer, texts were read and sung from all the great religions and bodies of wisdom. Gandhi was a great friend of Jesus and his pacifism in the Sermon on the Mount. He is my role model because he essentially embodied religious tolerance. This tolerance has ancient Indian roots. India is home to Hindus, Muslims, Christians, Sikhs, Jains, Buddhists, Zoroastrians, Jews, agnostics, and atheists who live together peacefully – with few exceptions. India has many ethnic and religious minorities and hundreds of languages. Tibet is my homeland, but in a way I am also a son of secular India.

You will find Hindu temples, Muslim mosques, Christian churches, and Buddhist sacred sites alongside each other. I know that every now and then there are also serious cases of localized violence. But it would be wrong to generalize them. On the whole, Indian society is peaceful and harmonious. All faiths share the ancient Indian principle of non-violence, Ahimsa, which also brought Gandhi such great political success. It was the bedrock of peaceful coexistence. That is the practice of secular ethics beyond all religions. The modern world should follow its example!

I often feel like a modern advocate for this ancient Indian way of thinking. This conception of secularism can be immensely useful for all people, all religions, all cultures and doctrines of wisdom, and all societies.

The many interviews that the two of us have had over decades have also served to promote understanding of deeper human values and secular ethics. This can help people become better and more conscious human beings. But our common path is this: more mindfulness towards all life, including animals and plants. On your last television broadcast, we discussed the global destruction of the environment and I said that I sometimes have the feeling that the Earth would be better off without people.

Franz Alt:

Every day, we drive 150 species of plants and animals to extinction, expand the deserts by 50,000 hectares, and spew 150 million metric tons of greenhouse gases into the air. Essentially, we are fighting a World War Three against nature. Religions have not been able to stop this development. 2014 was the warmest year on record. The Himalayan glaciers and the polar ice caps are melting. What can secular ethics accomplish in these circumstances? What are the core tenets of secular ethics?

Dalai Lama:

Mindfulness, education, respect, tolerance, caring, and nonviolence. We have achieved great material advances over the past century. That was generally positive. But those material advances are also what has led to the environment's current destruction. Now, in the twenty-first century, we need to learn, cultivate, and apply more inner values on all levels. A realistic look at the problems of our time, some of which you just listed, shows very clearly that we must find a sustainable and universal entry point to questions of ethics, inner values, and personal integrity – an entry point that will ultimately allow us to transcend cultural, ethnic, and religious differences. The principle of global responsibility is a key element of my concept of secular ethics. You are right, it comes down to the survival of our species. For me, this search for a truly sustainable and universal path is the basis for developing secular ethics.

Both theistic and non-theistic religions are primarily about the human spirit, about humans' spiritual well-being. That requires an intact environment, but also values like benevolence, forgiveness, and sincerity. In the past these values have been justified almost exclusively by religion. Cultivating these values has been part of every religious practice. But I see with ever greater clarity that our spiritual well-being depends not on religion, but on our innate human nature, our natural affinity for benevolence, compassion, and caring for others. Regardless of whether or not we belong to a religion, we all have a fundamental and profoundly human wellspring of ethics within ourselves. We need to nurture that shared ethical basis. Ethics, as opposed to religion, are grounded in human nature. And that is how we can work on preserving the environment. That is religion and ethics put into practice. Empathy is the basis of human coexistence. I believe human development relies on cooperation and not competition. That is scientifically proven.

We must learn now that humanity is all one big family, to which atheists, too, and the growing number of agnostics belong. We are all brothers and sisters: physically, mentally, and emotionally. But we are still focusing far too much on our differences instead of our commonalities. After all, every one of us is born the same way and dies the same way. It doesn't make much sense to take pride in our nations and religions – all the way to the graveyard!

(At this point, he laughs one of his famous long and gurgling Dalai Lama laughs!)

If all seven billion first considered what unites them and not what divides them, they would have less stress and less anger. We should learn that we are all friends. As I see it, I don't have any enemies, only people I haven't met yet. The young people of today have many more opportunities to get to know each other globally – and they should take advantage of them to work on improving the world. Compassion and love have been neglected far too much in education. We can and must change that now.

There are two viewpoints on human nature. One believes that humans are naturally violent, inconsiderate, and aggressive. The other believes that we have a natural tendency towards benevolence, harmony, and a peaceful life. I subscribe to the second viewpoint. That is why, in my opinion, ethics are not a collection of commandments and prohibitions to abide by, but a natural inner offering that can bring happiness and satisfaction to ourselves and others. I am personally driven by the simple desire to contribute to the greater good of humankind and all living creatures.

Ethical education starting around age 14 is more important than religion. Education changes everything. Human beings are capable of learning. In Germany, this was demonstrated by the fall of the Berlin Wall, an unforgettable experience for me, or the policies of the European Union after World War Two. Today, countries that were once enemies in wartime are building a peaceful Europe together. The EU even received the Nobel Peace Prize for that. Quite rightly!

Franz Alt:

I was there in Berlin in fall 1989 when ecstatic people lifted you onto the Wall, which had just been opened up. You were carrying a candle and said, »Just as Germany is being reunited now, Tibet will someday be free.« Do you still believe that?

Dalai Lama:

Certainly. All people strive for freedom. Of course I cannot specify a date. We need patience. That is another part of secular ethics.

Franz Alt:

Of the six billion believers in the world, there are many – especially in Europe – who do not take their own religions seriously. In Christianity, we call them »Christians by baptismal certificate.«

Dalai Lama:

Unfortunately, the six billion believers in the world include many corrupt people who only pursue their own interests. You are right, my dear friend. The twenty-first century must be shaped by inner values. Then our century will become the century of peace and dialogue. However, there won't be external peace until there is more inner peace. That applies to all current conflicts: in Ukraine, in the Middle East, in Afghanistan, and in Nigeria. Before there is »external disarmament,« there must be »inner disarmament.« Almost everywhere, religious fundamentalism is one of the causes of war. We know full well today that risking nuclear war would be tantamount to suicide. That alone shows that we are all interdependent and that we need to develop secular ethics in a globalized world.

In order to achieve worldwide secular ethics, of course we first need worldwide research. On that point I agree with many academics, particularly brain researchers, neuropsychologists, and educators. Modern neurobiology research suggests that altruistic and less egotistical behavior pays off for *everyone*. People don't necessarily have to act egotistically. They can also act altruistically, grasp things that are foreign to them, and focus on other people's well-being. But that will require even more education. The more strongly people believe that other people also act altruistically, the more likely they are to act that way themselves. Altruism simply makes us happier!

In other words, happiness is not just a matter of good luck, it's an ability that all people hold within themselves. Everyone can be or become happy. Modern science has shown us which factors facilitate happiness and which factors prevent us from being happy. We can transform the factors that prevent our happiness step by step. That holds for individuals, but also for society. The goal of secular ethics is to liberate us from both temporary and long-term suffering and to cultivate our ability to promote other people's pursuit of happiness as well. One aspect of compassion is being prepared to act spontaneously for the sake of others.

To be sure, secular ethics requires training of the heart, plenty of patience, and persistent effort. It's also clear that for secular ethics to be truly helpful, we need not only knowledge, but action. After all, we often know what to do but we don't do what we know.

Franz Alt:

You are a strong advocate of modern brain research. Why is that?

Dalai Lama:

Our brain is an organ of learning. Neuropsychology teaches us that we can exercise our brains like muscles. So by deliberately absorbing goodness and beauty, we can positively influence our brains and overcome negativity. Using the power of our minds, we can change our brains for the better. Those are revolutionary advances. Thanks to those advances, we also know better than before that ethics, compassion, and social behavior are inborn traits, but religion is acquired. We need to draw conclusions from that. Religions should as well. Ethics run deeper and are more natural than religion.

Franz Alt:

What questions do we need to ask ourselves in order to increase our compassion?

Dalai Lama:

Are we open-minded or narrow-minded? Have we considered the big picture or only aspects of it? Do we think and act holistically? Do we really take a long-term view of things, or more of a short-term view? Are our actions really motivated by sincere compassion? Is our compassion restricted to our own families, friends, whom we can generally identify with? We need to think, think, think. And research, research, research. Essentially, ethics is about our mental state and not our formal religious affiliation. We need to overcome our personal limitations and understand other people's points of view.

Twenty years ago I was still laughed at for being interested in this kind of research. Today it is receiving more and more recognition. Those who don't recognize altruism cannot understand how politics and markets really work. In the current Ukraine conflict, that means: Eastern Europe needs Western Europe and Western Europe needs Eastern Europe. So, talk to each other. Realize that today, in the age of globalization, we live in one world. Our new philosophy must be »Your interests are our interests.« Fundamentalism is always harmful. Yesterday's concepts won't help us anymore. Especially for children, who are the adults of tomorrow, ethics are more important than religion.

Climate change, too, can only be solved on a global scale. I hope and pray that this realization will finally bring tangible results at the next climate summit in Paris in late 2015. In general, egotism, nationalism, and violence are the wrong path. The most important question we can ask for a better world is »How can we serve each other?« To make that shift, we need to sharpen our awareness. The same holds true for politicians. We need to maintain positive states of mind. I practice that four hours per day. Meditation is more important than ritualized prayer. Children should learn morals and ethics. That's more important than any religion.

Franz Alt:

Does the practice of meditation have measurable biological effects?

Dalai Lama:

For a while now, Western researchers have been conducting neurological studies of Tibetans who have been meditating for a long time. To summarize the results briefly, meditation is good for physical and psychological health, for satisfaction and well-being. That has also been my personal experience.

Franz Alt:

How important is happiness for the development of secularized ethics?

Dalai Lama:

Well, all seven billion people want to be happy – and we have the right to be, for we all live on the same planet, breathe the same air, and eat from the same soil. Likewise, my future always depends on other people and other people's futures depend on mine. The climate catastrophe we are facing reminds us of this connection. Which of us could live alone in the desert? I ask that question to audiences at my talks all around the world. If we encounter someone in the solitude of the desert, the last thing we'd ask is their religion or nationality. If I am alone in the desert, it doesn't much matter that I'm His Holiness, the Dalai Lama. It wouldn't help me whatsoever!

(He has another long and loud laugh.)

Needless to say, I make mistakes too. I eat too many sweets, for instance, so I'm in danger of being reincarnated as a bee!

(He laughs loudly.)

I'm not a god. I'm just one person out of more than seven billion. That's also why I never feel lonely. As a human being, my first ambition is to help other people. That's what true friendship and humanity are about: relieving other people's suffering. And that's why all religions preach love, tolerance, and forgiveness.

Whether people accept religion is a question of their personal attitudes and decisions. The goal of all religions is to make us better and happier people. That's why we should have respect and appreciation for each other. That also creates mutual harmony.

My Muslim friends tell me that violent Muslims aren't real Muslims. Weapons cannot create true peace anywhere in the world. I find wars in the name of religion difficult to stomach. Neither can I understand why Germany and France are among the biggest arms exporters in the world. Weapons lead to murder and homicide. Without weapons, wars couldn't be waged. The primary causes of war and violence are our negative emotions. We give them too much space and give too little space to our intellect and our compassion.

I suggest more listening, more contemplation, more meditation. I agree with Mahatma Gandhi: »Be the change you want to see in the world.«

In some totalitarian countries, we see that peace can only last if human rights are respected, if people have food to eat, and if individuals and communities are free. We can only achieve true peace within, among, and around ourselves by first achieving inner peace. Another part of happiness is developing a universal sense of responsibility and a set of secular ethics.

Franz Alt:

Can people become happy at all in the face of death?

Dalai Lama:

That is certainly a fascinating question as well as a central one. There are people who do not or do not want to know that they will die. And there are people who have forgotten that they are alive. Compassion for ourselves means turning our attention to death in order to enrich our lives. If we accept death as part of life, we protect ourselves from frittering away our time with meaningless distractions. Watching the sunset, we can ask ourselves: Will I live to see the sunrise again tomorrow morning? But we can also ask ourselves: What if death is only a transitional stage and our spirits will pass through other states of being in the future? By asking these questions, we can learn to take a selfless and peaceful attitude and to let go of both our possessions and what we love. A selfless and detached attitude is the best and smartest preparation for death.

Life is short. If we succumb to negative emotions, we squander it. Whenever I feel a certain sense of frustration or too much sadness, I meditate on these lines by Shantideva, an Indian Buddhist master from the seventh century:

For as long as space remains,
For as long as sentient beings remain,
Until then may I too remain
To dispel the miseries of the world.

When I contemplate these lines, my feeling of frustration flies away. Suffering can provide real training for life. You can see that if you look at the life stories of prominent people.

Franz Alt:

What can each of us do for a better and more peaceful world?

Dalai Lama:

All religions have the duty to guide people to internal and external peace. If we want to make this world a better place, we need to become better people ourselves. There isn't a convenient path. We must start by seeing the humanity in our enemies. In the Sermon on the Mount, Jesus said »love thine enemy.« It's in our own interest for us to do everything we can for the well-being of all living creatures. To do that, we need to train our spirits and educate our hearts. After 1945, the EU chose the right path of cooperation between former enemies. Enemies became friends. That was only possible because millions of people pursued that path deliberately. NATO could move its headquarters to Moscow.

(He laughs.)

Then the Russians would see whether the West takes its friendship and its ideal of »love thine enemy« seriously. The true enemy is within us and not outside. External hostilities aren't permanent – and neither are those between China and Tibet. If you respect your enemies, they might become your friends one day.

For that reason, I will always stand by nonviolence. That means intelligently loving your enemy. Through intensive meditation, we will find that our enemies can become our best friends. By following purely secular ethics, we will become more easygoing, empathetic, and judicious people. Then there is a chance for the twenty-first century to be a century of peace, a century of dialogue, and a century of a more caring, responsible, and empathetic human race.

That is my hope. And that is my prayer. I eagerly look forward to the day when children will learn the principles of nonviolence and peaceful conflict resolution – in other words, secular ethics – at school.

Franz Alt:

I just thought of another question that I've wanted to ask you for a long time. Could the next Dalai Lama be a woman? You are for equal opportunity, aren't you?

Dalai Lama:

Why not? But she should be attractive.

(At this, he laughs especially loudly for a long time.)

Real equality and equal opportunity between women and men are critical for a better world. This is another area where all religions have some catching up to do. It's a crucial aspect of secular ethics. And also a question of justice and compassion. Many women are ahead of us men in developing inner values.

Franz Alt:

What do you mean by inner values?

Dalai Lama:

According to our biological nature, we are animals that thrive in an environment of compassion, caring, affection, and warm-heartedness. I'm thinking of my own mother. The essence of compassion is the desire to alleviate others' suffering and promote their well-being. Women are somewhat better than us men when it comes to developing these inner values such as benevolence, patience, forgiveness, generosity, and tolerance. Major problems such as wars and environmental destruction or wasting resources are primarily male problems. They are the result of indifference. But we all have a basic predisposition for developing inner values like awareness and mindfulness. I don't want to convert anyone, but I am mainly preoccupied by the desire to contribute to the good of humanity.

Franz Alt:

I have noticed that you have been promoting the Buddhist ideal of mindfulness all around the world for a long time. Why is mindfulness so important in this day and age?

Dalai Lama:

Far too much stock is placed in material values. They are important, but they will not reduce our stress, anxiety, fear, anger, or frustration. We must overcome these mental burdens. That is why we need a deeper level of thinking. That's what I call mindfulness, a deeper level of thinking and feeling, and it's very important to that end.

Mindfulness is irrespective of whether a person is a believer or a nonbeliever. That's immaterial; all of us are only people with the same emotions and the same sort of intelligence. Some of our emotions are very, very destructive. They destroy not only our peace of mind, but eventually our health as well. Some scientists have found that peace of mind is extremely important for health. According to those medical scientists, anger, hatred, and fear eat up our immune systems. That is why having a quiet mind is so very important.

As I always say, there are seven billion human beings and all of them have the same potential. All of them are the same, mentally, emotionally, and physically. So they all have the ability to use their intelligence properly. It always comes down to clarity of mind. We should analyze what is useful for our health and what is harmful. Then we should sort out what we know: this is something healthy and that is something harmful. The same goes for our emotions. Some emotions are good for our health and our peace of mind, while others are very destructive. With clear knowledge, everyone can tell them apart. Then we will develop the ability to reduce destructive emotions and increase constructive emotions.

Through meditation and contemplation we can learn, for example, that patience is the most potent antidote for anger, satisfaction for greed, bravery for fear, and understanding for doubt. It is not very helpful to rage against others. Instead, we should strive to change ourselves.

This, I believe, applies to all seven billion people, both believers and atheists. I hope that with our many conversations, we make a small contribution towards promoting happiness and overcoming suffering.

Franz Alt:

What is the essence of all religions?

Dalai Lama:

Love! There is no question. People who believe in God, the creator, practice love. Many Christian brothers and sisters have really dedicated their lives to serving others, particularly poor people. All of that comes out of the teachings of love. That said, there are big differences between religions' philosophies. In my opinion, these different philosophical views are simply different methods, different approaches for promoting love. The kernel of all religions is love. Loving our neighbor is more pleasant for all of us than hating what is different. We prefer other people to be generous as opposed to vicious. And who wouldn't rather be treated with tolerance, respect, and mercy than with closed-mindedness, disrespect, and antagonism?

I am deeply convinced that we can all develop our inner values, which don't contradict any religion, but which also – crucially – don't depend on any religion. I therefore hope that we come to more and more ethical awareness and thereby experience a transformation of values in the near future.

I don't want to dictate any moral values – that wouldn't serve anyone. All true progress needs to be voluntary and freely chosen. That's the only way to achieve the happiness we are all striving for. But, in light of the problems of our time, it is no longer enough to ground ethics in religious values. Rather, it is time to clear a new path, aside from religion, for our understanding of spirituality and ethics in the globalized world.

I am not a scientist. But since I have lived in exile – which, as you see, also has its advantages – I have met scientists from all over the world: physicists, biologists, cosmologists, psychologists, and recently also neurobiologists and neuropsychologists.

I have seen for myself that today, happiness is in the research lab. Ethics is the study of happiness. That is gratifying to me. We can learn that happiness is the outcome of inner maturity. And I am learning that there is much common ground between modern science and old religious values such as conscious compassion, loving benevolence, and mindfulness. Science teaches us today that true happiness is not only possible, it is our birthright. So as science is opening up more and more to religion, religion is also opening up to science.

Pope Benedict XVI was on the same page when he called for greater communication between faith and reason. Many thinkers and philosophers have long seen religions as more of an obstacle to the pursuit of knowledge – often rightly so – but today this relationship is changing for the better. The rise of computers and IT will continue to accelerate this change even further. In the age of globalization, tolerance has better prospects than ever.

Franz Alt:

A hundred years ago, humanity experienced the outbreak of World War One, which claimed 17 million lives, followed by 50 million dead in World War Two. Do you believe humanity has learned from these disasters? Will the twenty-first century be the century of peace?

Dalai Lama:

Sure. I believe that people, especially Europeans, know the meaning of war. Many older people in

Germany still remember quite clearly how destructive that was. The same goes for Japan. That is why I believe that both nations, Germany and Japan, as well as most people everywhere, oppose violence.

I have had the opportunity to visit a large number of countries and meet people. Everywhere I go, I think the desire for peace is very clear. Take the Iraq War, for example. There were protests against it from Australia to the United States, but also in Germany and France.

Now humanity seems to be maturing somewhat. The desire for peace and the rejection of violence are very strong. We need to make worldwide efforts to stop, contain, or eliminate all violent methods. It is not enough anymore to tell people that we oppose violence and want peace.

We must use more effective methods. Arms exports are obviously a major impediment to building peace. I simply don't understand why Germany and France are among the biggest arms exporters in the world. Without weapons, wars couldn't be waged.

Whenever we face difficulties or there is an economic crisis, or even when religious disputes arise, we must work towards a model where the only correct method is dialogue.

We must learn that we are all brothers and sisters. I often say that the past century was the century of violence. This twenty-first century should be the century of dialogue! We can never change the past, but we can always learn from it to create a better future.

The idea that problems can be solved with violence and weapons is a disastrous delusion. With rare exceptions, violence always leads to more violence. In our interconnected world, war is an anachronism that contradicts reason and ethics. The Iraq War, which George W. Bush began in 2003, was a catastrophe. This conflict still hasn't been resolved to this day and has claimed the lives of many people.

It is plainly not enough to appeal to politicians' desire for peace. It is more important for increasing numbers of people throughout the world to speak out for disarmament. Disarmament is compassion put into practice. But the prerequisite for external disarmament is an inner disarmament of hatred, prejudice, and intolerance. I appeal to all current warring parties: »Don't arm yourselves! Disarm!« And to all people: »Overcome hatred and prejudice with understanding, cooperation, and tolerance!«

Franz Alt:

What is the most important goal for the younger generation in the future?

Dalai Lama:

I believe that both of us, dear friend – the generation of the twentieth century – have created a lot of problems. Now let the generation of the twenty-first century solve these problems. Peacefully, though dialogue. So the young generation is very important. The past is past. The twenty-first century is only 15 years old; the remaining 85 years are yet to come. There are many opportunities to create a better world, to bring about a change in thinking: at the family level, the community level, the national level, or the international, global level. As I see it, we can achieve this primarily through education. Violent methods are outdated. Representatives of the media like yourself, but also teachers and parents, play critical roles in education and awareness.

Franz Alt:

When you think about the relationship between China and Tibet in the long run, are you optimistic? If so, why?

Dalai Lama:

Yes, I'm optimistic. Why? Look, we have lived side by side for a thousand years. At times in the past the relationship was very friendly, for instance through marriage or for other reasons. And sometimes we would fight. In the seventh or eighth century, I think Tibet invaded China. The past is past. The future is more important. And I see a new development there. The Buddhist population in China proper is now over 400 million people. Many of those Chinese Buddhists are really showing genuine interest in Tibetan Buddhism and many of them follow its teachings.

Accordingly, many Chinese and Japanese Buddhists appreciate our knowledge. We have noticed that over the past three or four years, around a thousand articles about Tibet have been written by Chinese authors in the Chinese language. All thousand articles fully support our approach. They take a very critical stance towards their own government's policy. In my opinion, that is a clear sign that many Chinese support our political objective.

Over the past few years, I have met several thousand Chinese – students, teachers, and businesspeople as well intellectuals and writers. Many of them are really showing concern about Tibet and solidarity with us. Meanwhile, the top political leaders are becoming more realistic. Even Communist leaders are now speaking favorably about Buddhism. That is something quite new. So things are changing. I am convinced that peace between China and Tibet is possible.

Notwithstanding all the suffering that China has brought upon us Tibetans for decades, I am still convinced that most human conflicts can be resolved through sincere dialogue carried out in a spirit of openness and reconciliation. This strategy of nonviolence and reverence for all life is Tibet's gift to the world.

After all, both of our peoples have lived alongside one another largely in peace for over two thousand years. I would like to help restore this state of affairs. Violence always causes more violence, as we have experienced in Iraq and the entire Middle East for decades. But peace is likewise possible in the Middle East and Ukraine. The problems everywhere were made by humans. Therefore humans can also solve the problems.

However, patience, forbearance, humility, and generosity are essential components of secular ethics. In my travels I have found that the virtues of patience and contentment are more prominent in less developed countries where material hardship is widespread than in materially rich countries. True patience requires great inner strength. There are three aspects of patience: patience towards those who cause us suffering, acceptance of suffering, and acceptance of reality. This patience leads to a process of transformation and growth.

Franz Alt:

What is the current status of human rights in Tibet?

Dalai Lama:

Difficult. Very difficult. Among the Chinese officials, there are still many hard-liners holding important positions. These hard-liners believe they can solve all problems by force and repression. That is totally wrong and unrealistic. I have seen that, across the world, the use of force has never solved any problems.

In the case of Tibet, they have now been using force for 60 years. But more force also brings more resistance. And the Communist leaders still don't recognize that precisely that is the problem. Nevertheless, there are indications that the Chinese public as well as several political leaders are beginning to see that the current policy of repression is counterproductive. They are contemplating a more realistic approach. So, we will see. But it is still too soon to say definitely. Meanwhile, the people suffer immensely. Not in terms of starvation or such things but anxiety, inordinate fear, too much sadness. That's why these self-immolations happen.

Franz Alt:

During the past six years, 137 Tibetans have committed suicide by self-immolation. What is your opinion of these acts of self-destruction?

Dalai Lama:

Of course they are very, very sad. These are dramatic, drastic actions. I don't know how much of an effect they have on the hard-liners. There is more anger, more repression, and in a number of cases their family members are arrested. It is a very sensitive political issue. As of 2015, there are over two thousand political prisoners in Tibet. Even though I totally retired from political responsibilities in 2011, the political hard-liners in China still manipulate everything that I say. They consider me a demon. So they have to manipulate every word from the demon's mouth …

I prefer to keep quiet. When I talk, I stick to prayers, only prayers. And of course my subject of secular ethics. I know some people in the Chinese leadership are interested in that too.

Franz Alt:

Most of these suicides were monks. Is suicide compatible with Buddhism?

Dalai Lama:

That depends on the motivation. Most Tibetans don't consider the self-immolations to be suicide. They see them as acts of radical political resistance in order to bring about a change in China's repressive policies in Tibet. I have appealed to the Chinese leadership and the international community to investigate the circumstances and causes of these self-immolations. But sadly, to no avail. I highly doubt whether this radical form of protest can have any impact.

Franz Alt:

Do you pray for the Communist leaders in Beijing?

Dalai Lama:

Certainly. They are also human beings. They also want happy lives.

(He laughs again.)

They are my brothers and sisters. So when I say seven billion, naturally they are included. And particularly those people who harbor anger, who have negative attitudes towards Tibet and towards me, they get a special prayer. I am a firm believer that Tibet will be free one day. Sooner or later, China will need to follow the worldwide trend towards democracy and freedom. In the long run, China cannot escape truth, justice and freedom either.

Franz Alt:

When Tibet is free, how do you envision its future?

Dalai Lama:

My hope and vision is for Tibet to become a demilitarized zone of peace and nonviolence between the two major powers of China and India.

My homeland now has major environmental problems. The reason the ecological problems are so serious is because Tibet is the upland that is the source of all the great rivers of Asia such as the Brahmaputra, the Yellow River, the Ganges, and the Mekong. And if this area is contaminated, that has negative consequences for two billion people. We know that nuclear waste is stored in some regions of Tibet. Certainly there also atom bombs stationed in parts of Tibet as well. Needless to say, nuclear power plants have a negative impact on the environment. Tibet's forests are also being clear-cut, causing widespread deforestation. Meanwhile, mineral resources are being rapidly exploited and depleted.

That is why I have a vision of transforming Tibet into an Ahimsa Zone – a zone of nonviolence – which includes a ban on the production, testing, and storing of nuclear and other weapons, and also of turning the Tibetan highlands into the largest nature preserve in the world. Additionally, nuclear power and other technologies that produce hazardous waste should not be used in Tibet in the future.

Franz Alt:

You have long accused China of a kind of »cultural genocide« in Tibet. What does that mean in concrete terms?

Dalai Lama:

From eyewitness accounts, we know that 1.2 million Tibetans died between 1950 and 1983. Those 1.2 million include Tibetans who died in Chinese prisons or in conflicts with Chinese troops or who starved to death because of China's failed economic policy in Tibet. Many also committed suicide out of desperation about the Chinese occupation.

Today there is a grave threat to the survival of Tibetan culture, language, religion, and identity due to the massive influx of Han Chinese to Tibet and the systematic policy of discriminating against the Tibetan language and severely restricting the study and practice of Buddhism.

Franz Alt:

Do you see any chance of returning to Tibet?

Dalai Lama:

Oh yes, dear friend. Things are changing.

Franz Alt:

But you are already almost 80 years old!

Dalai Lama:

That's true. If I die this year, then I will not see Tibet again. But if I live another five, ten, fifteen, or twenty years, for sure!

Franz Alt:

What age do you hope to live to?

Dalai Lama:

I had a dream I would reach age 113. My doctor says I will definitely reach 100. As you see, I still have plans.

(He slaps his thigh laughing.)

More information: *www.dalailama.com*, *www.franzalt.com*

The Dalai Lama Story:

An Inspiring Life

Ever since 2011, the Dalai Lama has been only the Tibetans' spiritual leader: he retired from his political role in that year. His retirement concluded 500 years of Dalai Lama tradition – voluntarily. When in human history has there ever been such a voluntary abdication of power?

Over the course of our thirty meetings, I have never once heard him complain, even though circumstances in his Tibetan homeland have often seemed hopeless. In fact, he is always cheerful and prone to loud laughter. Despite all the suffering and injustice – Chinese politicians and journalists call him a liar and rail against the Dalai Lama »fan club« – he remains upbeat and optimistic. When I asked why he never got upset even in very difficult situations, he says, »Why should I get upset? Then I'd have to calm down again. And that would be much too exhausting.«

A colleague from Swiss radio told me she had interviewed the Dalai Lama in India. Back in Zurich, she played her piece for her colleagues. »We can't broadcast that,« they said. »He's constantly laughing.« So they dialed India and asked the Dalai Lama's staff when he would be in Europe next – they wanted to interview him another time, but please without any laughter. »No problem,« said the assistant. »He'll be changing planes at the Frankfurt airport in three weeks. You can re-record the conversation there.«

So my colleague flew to Frankfurt and asked, »Please, Your Holiness, no laughing!« His Holiness didn't laugh a single time during the interview. But afterwards, when the recorder was switched off, he laughed for ten minutes straight. »My apologies,« he told the journalist. »I had to catch up. I simply cannot live without laughing!«

Puzzled, she asked, »Why do you have to laugh? What do you laugh about?« He answered, »I always think about all the crazy things we humans get up to on this Earth. And it's often hilarious!«

There are six principles that he considers fundamental. First comes the most important principle, nonviolence. Under his leadership, this has become a symbol of the struggle to free Tibet. At times he also quotes Jesus's dictum »love thine enemy« from the Sermon on the Mount. Second, and just as essential for him, is tolerance. »No peace among the nations without peace among the religions,« he says, citing the global ethos of Hans Küng.

The third principle: accept every religion in its uniqueness. Fourth: when I asked him in our last television interview what religion means today, the Pope of the East replied, »A religious person is someone who collaborates in preserving the Earth.« He points to the increasingly urgent issue of water throughout the Himalayas: »It's a question of survival for two billion people.«

He occasionally has trouble with the fifth principle of patience, he admits with a conspiratorial chuckle. Even he needs to work on that one. To be sure, he has plenty of opportunities to practice in his dealings with Chinese politicians. Another laugh.

He even cracks jokes about his sixth principle, death and rebirth. He has no clue what will happen after death, he says. »If I wind up in hell, I will definitely apply for vacation, because I'll want to know how things are going here on Earth.«

Unlike any other modern politician, the Dalai Lama has an almost childlike faith in political miracles: »One day we will cooperate well with China.« Upon receiving a skeptical reaction, he points to the miraculous friendship between German and France or the reconciliation between Germany and Poland. »It's clear to see, there's another way!«

He pins his greatest hope on two segments of the Chinese population: young people and the 400 million who believe in and practice Buddhism. In his view, Chinese Communism is an enormous spiritual void. »What are 65 years of Communism compared to 1,300 years of Tibetan Buddhism?« asks the monk from Lhasa.

The »Roof of the World« is the battleground for an almost unbelievable mental sparring match between the world's most religious nation and its most materialistic ideology. The future of the world rests in the outcome. Some might think it a case of David versus Goliath. But the Tibetan counters: »We all know who won that time.«

Yet for the Dalai Lama, nonviolence is not the same as tiptoeing around the issues. As always, he insists on clarity of mind. He accuses the Chinese occupiers of cultural genocide and unparalleled cultural barbarity in the mountains. As Alexander Solzhenitsyn writes, »The holocaust that happened in Tibet revealed Communist China as a cruel and inhuman executioner – more brutal and inhuman than any other Communist regime in the world.«

Around six million Tibetans reside within Tibet's former borders. But Beijing has plans to settle up to 20 million Chinese there. The Dalai Lama repeatedly asks how desperate his countrypeople must be if, during the past four years, 135 Tibetans have set themselves on fire in protest against the Chinese occupation.

Asked how he remains in such good shape on the brink of his eightieth birthday, he replies with the inevitable laugh, »That's simple – no dinner for fifty years!« He goes to bed at 6:30 every night and sleeps until 3:30. Then he meditates until seven and eats breakfast before starting work.

The Dalai Lama is the personal embodiment of a number of ethical and spiritual values: resistance against the rule of violence, critique of capitalism (like the Pope), love of animals, advocacy for the environment, and opposition to nuclear weapons. This reads like a list of a left-wing Westerner's pet causes. But he refuses to be ideologically appropriated.

He is a victim of persecution and a winner of the Nobel Peace Prize. Some say he has achieved Enlightenment. He cannot be beaten in the war for souls. Incidentally, a German intellectual once asked him, »Your Holiness, how can I achieve Enlightenment quickly?« He answered, »The best thing to do is go to the doctor and get an injection.«

It was an experience not to be missed, in Hamburg in summer 2014. For four days in a row, 7,000 people crowded into the conference center to see him speak – twice a day. The Dalai Lama spoke up to five hours a day for four days without notes. Many people laughed, some cried, and everyone listened intently. How does the man do it? Well, he certainly has plenty to tell us.

Franz Alt

THE DALAI LAMA:

A LIFE IN DATES

1935: On 6 July, the future Dalai Lama was born to a farming family in the Tibetan village of Taktser and named Lhamo Dhondrub. At the age of two, he was recognized as the reincarnation of the Dalai Lama (»ocean of wisdom«), taken to Lhasa, and enthroned at age four and a half. As a Buddhist monk, he was given the name Tendzin Gyatsho. At six, he began his training in dialectics, Tibetan art and culture, linguistics, medicine, and Buddhist philosophy, his most important subject. He is considered to be the reincarnation of Chenrezig, the Buddha of Compassion.

1950: The Chinese People's Liberation army invaded Tibet and occupied the country. On 17 November, the fifteen-year-old Dalai Lama took over the task of governing.

1954: The Dalai Lama traveled to Beijing and participated in peace talks with Mao Zedong, Zhou Enlai, and Deng Xiaoping – without success.

1959: On 10 March, the Tibetans launched an uprising against foreign rule, provoking a bloody crackdown by the Chinese. Some 90,000 Tibetans lost their lives. The Dalai Lama fled to India and founded a government-in-exile in Dharamsala. Hundreds of thousands of Tibetans escaped the perils of their homeland and sought refuge around the world, an exodus that is still ongoing.

1966–1976: During China's Cultural Revolution, almost all 6,000 monasteries were destroyed.

1987: The Dalai Lama announced the »Middle Way.« According to this new approach, Tibet no longer sought independence from China, but rather autonomy within the Chinese state similar to the status of South Tyrol within Italy.

1989: The Dalai Lama was awarded the Nobel Peace Prize in Oslo. The Nobel Committee explained: »His Holiness has developed his philosophy of peace from a great reverence for all things living and upon the concept of universal responsibility embracing all mankind as well as nature.«

2010: In early March, tens of thousands of Tibetans worldwide demonstrated against China's violent occupation of the »Roof of the World.«

2011: The Dalai Lama handed over political leadership of Tibet to Lobsang Songay, who had been elected prime minister of the Tibetan government-in-exile. The Dalai Lama wanted to be a »simple monk« even though many Tibetans accorded him godlike status.

Between 2009 and April 2015, some 137 Tibetans committed self-immolation (suicide by burning) in protest against China's repressive policies in Tibet.

2015: A quote from one of his bodyguards: »I have nothing to do – everyone loves him!«

Will the 14th Dalai Lama be the last? In many interviews he has stated that the institution of the Dalai Lama should end with him. He fears that China's Communist Party would want to appoint the next Dalai Lama itself. He seeks to prevent that. In the past, high-ranking monks have identified the Dalai Lama, but now Communist officials have said that their party has the right to determine the religious process of reincarnation. Beijing accuses the Dalai Lama of destroying »the normal order of Tibetan Buddhism.« In doing so, China's Communist Party wants to move beyond controlling births and start controlling rebirths. When Communists become pious...

In reality, there is no doubt that after more than 60 years of Communist rule over Tibet, almost all Tibetans honor the Dalai Lama as their religious leader and wish for his return.

About the Author: Franz Alt

Dr. Franz Alt is a television journalist and best-selling author.

Born in 1938 in Bruchsal, Germany, he studied political science, history, theology, and philosophy and completed his doctorate in 1967 with a dissertation on Konrad Adenauer. For 35 years, he was a writer, reporter, and host (of the shows Report, Zeitsprung, and Querdenker) for Erstes Deutsche Fernsehen, Germany's principal publicly owned television channel. His books have been translated into 12 languages with editions numbering over 2.2 million copies. His honors have included the Goldene Kamera, the Bambi, the Adolf Grimme Award, the German and European Solar Award, the Human Rights Award, membership in the German Speakers' Hall of Fame, and the Most Extraordinary Orator in Germany of 2011.

Franz Alt gives talks worldwide and writes for 40 newspapers.

His Holiness, the Dalai Lama, the television journalist Dr. Franz Alt, and Benevento Publishing will be donating all royalties and profit from this little book to German Aid to Tibetans.